The Story of King David

by Martina Smith

illustrated by Peter Grosshauser
and Ed Temple

SPARK
HOUSE
FAMILY

MINNEAPOLIS

Long ago, in the land of the Hebrew people, a boy named Samuel was born. God had something special planned for Samuel. His mother had prayed to God to bring her a son. She promised God that her son would serve God well.

When Samuel was still a boy, his mother took him to the temple. The temple was a special place where the Hebrew people worshipped God. Samuel helped take care of a priest named Eli, who was nearly blind.

Samuel grew and grew, serving God every day of his life. One night, something special happened in the temple.

As Samuel slept, he heard a voice call out, "Samuel." Samuel thought it was Eli calling, so he jumped out of bed.

"Here I am," Samuel answered as he ran to Eli. "I'm here because you called me."

Eli shook his head. "I didn't call you. Go back to bed."

Samuel did as he was told. A little while later, the voice called again, "Samuel."

This time, Samuel crawled out of bed and went to Eli, yawning. Eli again told Samuel that he hadn't called. "Now please go back to bed," Eli said.

When this happened a third time, Eli thought it must be God calling Samuel. Eli told Samuel, "If you are called again, just say, 'God, I hear you and I will do whatever you want.'"

When the voice called again, Samuel did as Eli told him. It was God! And God spoke to Samuel about many things.

With God's help, Samuel grew up to share many messages from God. People all over Israel came to know Samuel as God's trusted prophet.

When Samuel was older, God said to him, "I want you to anoint a new king. Bring a horn filled with oil to Bethlehem and look for Jesse and all his sons. One of his sons will be the next king."

So Samuel walked to Bethlehem and found Jesse. "Line up all your sons," Samuel said.

Jesse's oldest son was big and strong. Samuel thought, "This must be the king."

But God said, "No, not that one."

One by one, the sons came forward to see if they would be chosen.

And one by one, God said, "NO, not this one." God was looking at the inside, not at size and strength.

Finally they ran out of sons—except for one. Jesse's son David was outside watching the sheep. They called for him.

David came inside. He was just a boy, gentle and quiet. His eyes sparkled with joy.

Was David the one? A hush fell over the room.

"Yes!" God told Samuel.

"Yes!" Samuel told everyone. Samuel poured oil from the horn onto David's head, anointing him with God's love. David would be the next king!

At this time, King Saul ruled Israel. There came

a time when he and his army were fighting

the Philistines. In the valley between

the two armies stood Goliath,

the biggest man Saul had

ever seen.

"Who will fight me?" Goliath roared, waving his spear and sword.

Saul and his army were afraid. They could not beat Goliath. They could not win against the Philistines. Surely they would be captured and become slaves.

"Send out your best warrior," Goliath ordered. "Let him fight against me. If I win, you will be our slaves. If your soldier wins, we will serve you and your God."

Saul waited. No one stepped forward to take Goliath's challenge. Then Saul felt a small tug on his sleeve. Looking down, he saw David, the young shepherd boy.

"I will do it, King Saul," David said. "I will fight Goliath."

"You are a boy. How can you beat a gigantic man like Goliath?" Saul turned to go.

"Wait, King Saul," David said. "God protects me from the wolves and bears that go after my sheep. God will protect me now too."

David reached down and picked up five smooth stones. In his right hand he carried the same sling he used to chase away the wolves and wild animals. Saul patted David's head and pointed down the rocky path leading to the valley.

Goliath laughed when he saw David. "You are the warrior they send out against me?"

David slipped his hand into his pouch and selected a stone. "I am not afraid of your spear and sword, Goliath," David said. "God will help me." David rushed toward Goliath, swinging his sling. The smooth stone flew through the air and hit Goliath in the forehead.

Down, down, down Goliath fell. Down fell his sword. Down fell his spear. Down fell his mighty shield.

David, the small shepherd boy, had beaten the mighty Goliath. King Saul and all his soldiers rose up with a shout!

When the Philistines saw that Goliath had fallen, they were afraid and ran away. Trusting in God gave David courage when he needed it most.

As he grew up, David wrote songs about God.

One of his songs says that God is like a shepherd.

God loves and cares for each and every one of us.

God is my shepherd, he gives me all I need.
He gives me wonderful places to rest and sleep.
He lets me splash and play in cool, clear waters.
He helps me do what is right.
I am not afraid even in the darkest nights
Because you are with me, God, and
Your protection comforts me.
When danger comes, you give me strength.
My life is filled with your love,
and all I want is to be
With you my whole life long.

David sang this song to his sheep, thankful

for all the ways God loved and cared

for him.

David became a great king for the Hebrew people. He lived in a beautiful palace. Outside was the old tent where people had worshipped God for years. David wanted to build a new temple for God's people. He began making plans.

"Wait," God said to David. "Someday I will have a great house, but not right now. After you are gone, your son will build my house."

David told his son Solomon about God's promise. "One day, you will build God's house."

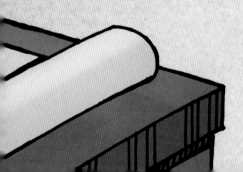

When Solomon became king, he began planning a new temple for God. He wanted it to be the most dazzling building ever built.

First, Solomon told his workers to dig large stones out of the ground.

"I don't want God to hear any loud building noises here," Solomon told the workers. "Measure, cut, and shape the stones out in the hills before you bring them here." The workers did what Solomon told them to do.

Next, Solomon told his workers to make the roof and floor out of a hard, sturdy wood called cedar.

Solomon had the workers decorate the temple with flower designs. He made a room especially for God and had it covered in gold. The room glowed and shimmered.

When the temple was finished, Solomon put a special box called the Ark of the Covenant into the room of gold. The people had put God's Ten Commandments in the box. Wherever the Ark of the Covenant was, God was there too.

The people went to the temple every day to worship God. God was happy to live in the temple that David's son had built.

Making Faith Connections: A Note to Adults

Sharing a Bible story with a child can be a wonderful time to grow your faith together. Here are a few suggestions for ways you can enrich a child's engagement and learning with this book.

Questions for Reflection

After reading the story together, ask your child these questions.

 What did God see in David that other people didn't? What would make him a good king?

 What would God see inside you that would make you a good leader like David?

 How was David able to bring down mighty Goliath, the Philistine?

 David wrote a song about how God loves us and stays with us, no matter what. How do you know that God loves and protects you all the time?

 The people worshipped God in the temple to feel close to God. Where do you feel close to God?

Activities

 Give your child a small, smooth stone to keep in their pocket. Tell them to touch it whenever they feel afraid. They can use it to help remember that God is with them.

Using olive oil or cooking oil, help your child draw a cross on the foreheads of your family members. Together, you are anointing them!

 Write your own song for God with your child, telling all about God. Sing your song to members of your family.

 Ask your child to draw or paint a picture of a beautiful temple or a place where they could go to worship God.

 Did you notice Squiggles, the expressive caterpillar who appears throughout the book? When you see Squiggles, after you read the text aloud, ask your child how Squiggles is feeling. Then ask why Squiggles feels that way. Invite your child to share about a time they felt the same way Squiggles does.

A Prayer to Say Together

Tell your child or children that you will say a rock prayer together. Choose a special rock and pass it around your prayer circle. When it is your turn, say thank you to God or ask God for something. Make sure everyone gets a chance. Help anyone who needs a prompt.

End the prayer time by saying together, "Thank you, God, for hearing our prayer. God, you ROCK! Amen!"

25 24 23 22 21 20 19 18 17 16   1 2 3 4 5 6 7 8 9 10

Hardcover ISBN: 978-1-5064-0226-0

E-book ISBN: 978-1-5064-0227-7

Cover design: Alisha Lofgren
Book design: Eileen Z. Engebretson

Library of Congress Cataloging-in-Publication Data

Smith, Martina, author.
  The story of King David : a spark Bible story / by Martina Smith ; illustrated by Peter Grosshauser and Ed Temple.
     pages cm. — (Spark bible stories)
  Summary: "This picture book shares the story of the young shepherd boy who became a great king"— Provided by publisher.
  Audience: Ages 3-7.
  Audience: K to grade 3.
  ISBN 978-1-5064-0226-0 (alk. paper)
1. David, King of Israel—Juvenile literature. 2. Samuel (Biblical judge)— Juvenile literature. 3. Goliath (Biblical giant)—Juvenile literature. 4. Bible stories, English—Samuel. I. Grosshauser, Peter, illustrator. II. Temple, Ed, illustrator. III. Title.
  BS580.D3S53 2015
  222'.4092—dc23
                                          2015025637

Printed on acid-free paper.

Printed in China

V63474; 9781506402260; FEB2016